The Life of St Francis

Anita Ganeri

Heinemann LIBRARY

www.heinemann.co.uk/library

Visit our website to find out more information about **Heinemann Library** books.

To order:

 Phone 44 (0) 1865 888066

 Send a fax to 44 (0) 1865 314091

Visit the Heinemann Bookshop at www.heinemann.co.uk/library to browse our catalogue and order online.

First published in Great Britain by Heinemann Library, Halley Court, Jordan Hill, Oxford OX2 8EJ, part of Harcourt Education.
Heinemann is a registered trademark of Harcourt Education Ltd.

Editorial: Lucy Thunder and Helen Cannons
Design: Richard Parker and Tinstar Design Ltd. (www.tinstar.co.uk)
Illustrations: Maureen Gray
Picture Research: Rebecca Sodergren and Liz Moore
Production: Edward Moore

Originated by Repro Multi-Warna
Printed and bound in China by South China Printing Company
The paper used to print this book comes from sustainable resources.

ISBN 0 431 18080 6 (hardback)
08 07 06 05 04
10 9 8 7 6 5 4 3 2 1

ISBN 0 431 18086 5 (paperback)
09 08 07 06 05
10 9 8 7 6 5 4 3 2 1

British Library Cataloguing in Publication Data
Anita Ganeri
The Life of St Francis. – (Life of saints)
271.3'02
A full catalogue record for this book is available from the British Library.

Acknowledgements
The publishers would like to thank the following for permission to reproduce photographs: Art Archive/Museo Nacional del Virreinato Tepotzotlan Mexico/Dagli Orti p 14; Bridgeman Art Library pp 20, 25; Corbis/Arte&Immagini srl p 23; Corbis/Dave Bartruff p 4; Corbis/Elio Ciol p13; Corbis/Danny Lehman p 15; Corbis/National Gallery Collection: by kind permission of the Trustees of the National Gallery, London p 9; Corbis/Lance Nelson p 19; Corbis/Sergio Pitamitz p 27; Corbis Sygma/Bergsaker Tore p 26; Mary Evans Picture Library pp 11, 17; Sonia Halliday Photography pp 5, 21; Scala p 6, 22, 24; Topham Picturepoint p 16.

Cover photograph of St Francis, on a stained-glass window in Selborne Church, Hampshire, reproduced with permission of Sonia Halliday Photographs and Laura Lushington.

The publishers would like to thank Fr. Martin Ganeri OP for his assistance in the preparation of this book.

Every effort has been made to contact copyright holders of any material reproduced in this book. Any omissions will be rectified in subsequent printings if notice is given to the publishers.

Disclaimer
All the Internet addresses (URLs) given in this book were valid at the time of going to press. However, due to the dynamic nature of the Internet, some addresses may have changed, or sites may have changed or ceased to exist since publication. While the author and Publisher regret any inconvenience this may cause readers, no responsibility for any such changes can be accepted by either the author or the Publisher.

Contents

What is a saint?   4

St Francis is born   6

Fun and fighting   8

Life changes for Francis   10

God calls Francis   12

A poor monk   14

Animal tales   16

On his travels   18

A Christmas crib   20

Seeing an angel   22

Francis dies   24

Feast Day of St Francis   26

Fact file   28

Timeline   29

Glossary   30

Find out more   31

Index   32

Words shown in the text in bold, **like this**, are explained in the glossary.

What is a saint?

In the **Christian** religion, people try to live a **holy** life. Some men and women are especially holy. The Christian Church calls them saints. Christians believe that saints are very close to God.

Some Christians pray to the saints to help them.

Some saints look after a country, or have a special interest in a group of people, such as doctors. They are called **patron saints**. This book is about St Francis, the patron saint of Italy and of animals.

St Francis was well known for his kindness to people and animals.

St Francis is born

Francis was born over 800 years ago in the city of Assisi, in Italy. He grew up in a wealthy family and had several brothers and sisters. His father was a rich cloth **merchant**.

This painting shows Francis's birth in Assisi.

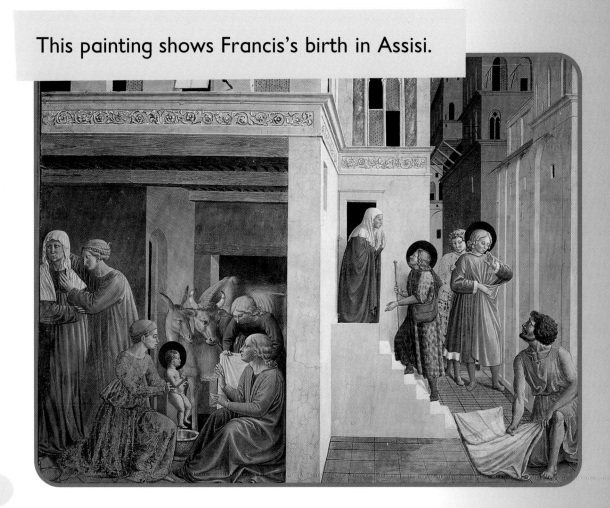

Francis went to school in Assisi. He learned to read and write the old language of **Latin**. He also learned to speak French. But Francis did not like school very much.

Fun and fighting

As a young man, Francis worked for his father. He liked going out and having fun with his friends. He was used to having fine clothes to wear and good food to eat.

When Francis was 20 years old, he became a soldier. He fought in a war between the two cities of Assisi and Perugia. He was caught and thrown into prison.

This painting shows Francis setting off to become a soldier.

9

Life changes for Francis

Later, two things happened that changed Francis's life. One day, he met a poor man who was dressed in rags. Francis felt sorry for him and gave the man his own fine clothes.

Next, he met a man who was a **leper**. Nobody went near the man in case they caught his illness. That did not frighten Francis, however. He went up to the man and kissed his hand.

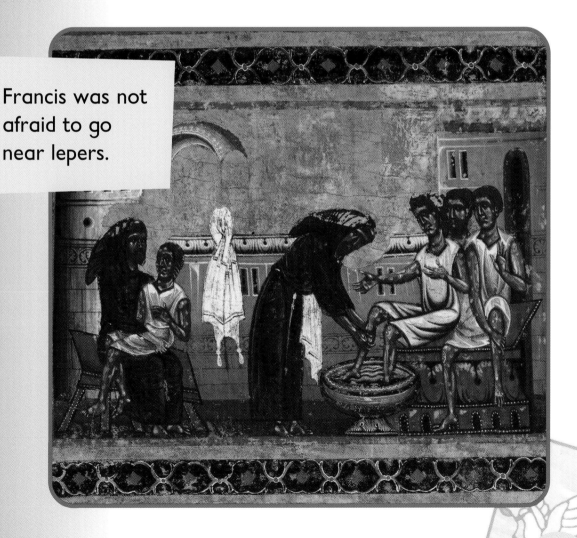

Francis was not afraid to go near lepers.

God calls Francis

Another day, Francis was in the ruined **chapel** of San Damiano. Suddenly, he heard a voice coming from the **crucifix**. It told him to find a way of repairing the chapel.

Francis rushed home and stole some of his father's finest cloth. He sold it and used the money to pay for the repairs. After this, Francis gave up his old life and did God's work.

This painting shows Francis selling his father's cloth.

A poor monk

Francis gave up his money and belongings. Instead of his rich clothes, he wore a rough, wool robe with a rope belt. From then on, he lived the life of a poor **monk**.

This statue shows Francis wearing his simple clothes.

People came from far and wide to hear Francis teaching about God. Many became monks like him. They lived near Assisi and led a hard life of work and prayer.

These monks are called Franciscans, after Francis.

Animal tales

Francis and his **monks** travelled all over Italy. Francis was very kind and gentle. He became famous for his love of animals. One story tells of how Francis **tamed** a fierce wolf.

Francis loved birds and other animals.

The hungry wolf lived near a town and killed the farmers' animals to eat. Francis made friends with the wolf and it stopped its attacks. In return, the townspeople gave it food.

This picture shows Francis taming the wolf.

On his travels

Francis wanted to travel to the Middle East to teach people about God. On the way, his ship was wrecked. Francis had to hide away on another ship to get back to Italy.

A few years later, Francis sailed to Egypt. The ruler of Egypt did not want to become a **Christian**, but he let Francis visit the **holy** Christian places in nearby Israel.

This is Jerusalem in Israel. Francis would have visited Jerusalem on his travels.

A Christmas crib

One Christmas, Francis went to the town of Greccio in Italy. He wanted to do something special to remember Jesus's birthday in Bethlehem. Then Francis had an idea.

Francis preparing the Christmas **crib** at Greccio in Italy.

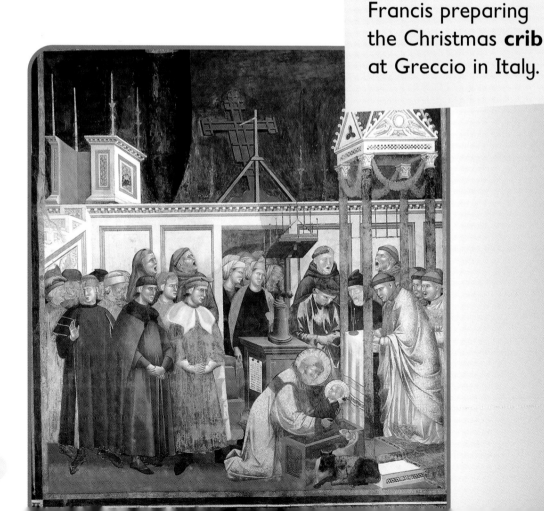

The **Bible** told how Jesus was born in a stable. So Francis made a model of the stable. Inside he put figures of Jesus, Mary and Joseph, the shepherds, the wise men, an ox and a donkey.

Today, at Christmas, most churches have a Christmas crib, like this one.

21

Seeing an angel

The next year, Francis went up in the mountains to pray. While he was there, he had an amazing dream. He saw an angel nailed to a cross, just as Jesus had been.

This is Mount La Verna in Italy, where Francis went to pray. It is a sanctuary, a holy place where people find peace.

When Francis woke up, he looked at his hands and feet. On each of them was a small mark, like a scar. These are called stigmata. They were like the marks left by the nails on Jesus's hands and feet.

This picture shows Francis receiving the stigmata. They are signs of his holiness.

Francis dies

Soon afterwards, Francis fell ill and almost went blind. He died in a **chapel** in his hometown of Assisi. Later, his body was buried in the beautiful **Basilica** of St Francis.

This is part of the inside of the Basilica of St Francis.

Francis lived a **holy** life. He worked hard to help other people and take care of the poor and needy. Two years after Francis's death, the pope made him a saint.

This scene shows Francis dying. St Francis's tomb is in the Basilica of St Francis, Assisi.

Feast Day of St Francis

On 4 October, many **Christians** all over the world celebrate the feast day of St Francis. This is the day after he died. They mark the day by saying prayers and remembering St Francis's life.

People all over the world celebrate St Francis's day. This elephant is taking part too!

People travel from far and wide to visit the places where Francis lived. Every year, thousands of **pilgrims** go to Assisi, Francis's hometown. They pray in the famous **basilica**.

Pilgrims come from all over the world to pray in the Basilica of St Francis.

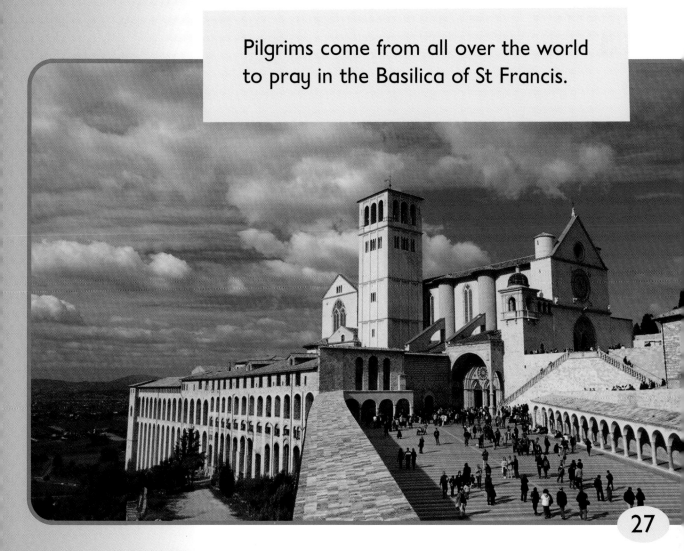

Fact file

- In pictures and statues, St Francis is usually shown dressed as a **monk**, with birds and animals around him.

- When he was born, Francis was named Giovanni (the Italian for John). But his father later called him Francesco (the Italian for Francis).

- St Francis is also the **patron saint** of **ecologists**, zoos, fire, families and **merchants**.

- In another story, one of St Francis's monks caught a fish to eat. But Francis put it back in the water and told it not to let itself get caught again. Instead of swimming off, the fish stayed near by to listen to Francis teach.

Timeline

- **1181 or 1182** Francis is born in Assisi, Italy
- **1202** Francis becomes a soldier. He fights in a war between the two cities of Assisi and Perugia.
- **1210** Francis's followers become known as Franciscan monks
- **1212** Francis travels to Palestine (now called Israel)
- **1219** Francis travels to Egypt and Israel to visit **Christian holy** places
- **1223** Francis makes a Christmas **crib** in Greccio, Italy
- **1224** The marks of the nails of the cross (stigmata) appear on Francis's hands and feet
- **1226** Francis dies in Assisi on 3 October
- **1228** Francis becomes a saint
- **1939** Francis becomes patron saint of Italy

Glossary

basilica large and splendid church

Bible the holy book of the Christian Church

chapel small church or part of a church

Christian someone who follows the teachings of Jesus Christ

crib model of the stable in which Jesus was born

crucifix cross with a figure of Jesus on it

ecologists people who study how plants and animals live in the wild

holy to do with God

Latin a very old language once spoken in Italy

leper person suffering from the disease leprosy. Their body is covered in sores.

merchant person who buys and sells things

monk man who belongs to a special religious group and lives a very holy life

patron saints saints who have special links with a country or group of people or animals. A patron is someone who looks after others.

pilgrims people who go on a journey to holy places linked to a saint's life

tame to make a wild animal calm and friendly

Find out more

Books

Brother Sun, Sister Moon: The Story of St Francis, Margaret Mayo (Orion, 2000)

Celebrations!: Christmas, Jennifer Gillis (Raintree, 2003)

Places of Worship: Catholic Churches, Clare Richards (Heinemann Library, 1999)

Places of Worship: Protestant Churches, Mandy Ross (Heinemann Library, 1999)

Websites

www.americancatholic.org/features/Francis/stories.asp
Stories about St Francis and his love of animals.

Index

animals 5, 16–17, 28
Assisi 6, 7, 9, 15, 24, 25, 27, 29
Christian religion 4, 14, 19, 26
Christmas crib 21, 29
churches and chapels 12, 20, 24, 27
death of St Francis 24, 26, 29
Franciscans 15, 29
Israel 19, 29
Italy 5, 6, 16, 20
kindness and holiness 11, 16–17, 23, 25
monks 14, 15, 16, 28, 29
patron saints 5, 28, 29
pilgrims 27
prayer 4, 22, 26
St Francis's Day 26
saints 4–5, 25, 28, 29
stigmata 23, 29